# HEARTSCAPES

The African Thinker
drawing, colour pencil

Cover and art: aquarelles
by Marion de Vos

Photo author: Hilde Vaatstra

Publisher: Demer Press, Belgium
www.lulu.com/content/10272085

ISBN: 978-1-4475-1864-8
Nur: 306

# HEARTSCAPES

## Poems

## Marion de Vos

Demer Press

# INTRODUCTION

Being the Chairman of the Worcester Museum Board in South Africa, I've met Marion de Vos and her husband Rob, Ambassador of the Netherlands, residing in Pretoria on a tour arranged by the Deputy Mayor of the Cape Winelands District Municipality Mr Clarence Johnson. While our Museum Manager Mr Tizzie Mangiagalli showed our honoured guests around, Marion was walking beside me and soon we talked about poetry. Two spirits connect and we started sending poems to each other.

Then we decided to publish our own poetry book DRIELUIK with Hilde Vaatstra who highlighted our poems with awesome photos. The book consists of Dutch, Afrikaans and English poems.

Marion invited me to do a PowerPoint presentation on the *Historic & Cultural relationship between The Netherlands and South Africa* on the 23rd April 2009 for the *International Diplomatic Spouses Association*. It was here that I've discovered that Marion is also a talented piano and an acoustic guitar player!

*HEARTSCAPES* is Marion's debut English poetry book published by Demer Press, Diepenbeek, in Belgium, 2011. What an honour and privilege to read through her poems. She hooked me with this lovely poem of nature titled *Summer* when she writes: "The wonder of nature's touch / is just a shiver on your skin." I saw the picture taken by her husband Rob of *The Paradise Widow* bird when she writes: "I pity this poor beauty, / trapped in his summer jail."

Her deep love for the sea is expressed in *Mother sea:* "My body stood / as an Aeolian harp / playing global tunes." Oh how can this lady play with words! So passionate! In *Lost paradise* she is expressing the helplessness of a sea creature everybody's craving for: "Abelone, heavenly name / of a lost paradise."

Like a story teller, she brings this poem home to the centre of the heart and touched mine - *The Streets of Bamako:* "the man screams inside / silently / like the horse / on the streets of Bamako." To hear the cry of the poorest of the poor.

A heartfelt sorrow can be heard while reading *Loss and gain (on leaving South Africa)*: "Loss cuts deep / but it will drain / through the channels / of new expectation."

In *HEARTSCAPES* you will find so much passion, metaphors, deep insight and wisdom while reading this highly recommendable poetry book, that you will never stop reading it over and over again!

Floris Brown

Swaziland

# Heartscapes

The road map to my heart
is strewn with love
for men and nature,
but also with hurt and pain
It is my * "carte du tendre".
If you want to know me,
follow its sinuous way
and * "if you don't know me
by now, you will never
ever know me."

* La carte du tendre - a 17th century French map of an imaginary land called
"Tendre"
* song by Simply Red

Mandela and Helen Suzman
(at her 90th Birthday)

**Nelson Mandela & Helen Suzman
on the occasion of her 90th birthday**


A photograph
in shades of brown
slowly fading
like old people do
but not their fame.

Togetherness
in tender embrace
black and white
like soul mates do
without fear.

Compassion
to crush aggression
with love
like great people do
following their heart.

Fragile
but strong enough
to bend and not break
like old people do
touching your soul.

Reconciliation
live to see it happen
the wonder of forgiving
like we all should do
for our children's sake.

**For Vicky,**

Vicky, my Fijian friend
behind your ear
a frangipani flower,
coming down
without fear
from your spiritual tower,
to make us see
me and my peer
our very inner power.
When awareness
comes near
it is your finest hour.
Unconditional love
for everything that's dear
falls like a healing shower,
cleansing our suspicious minds,
yielding a tear,
never will we turn sour.

## The Koi and the Hadeda


Slipping and sliding
silvery Koi cleave the water
from reed to stone.

Green grass is the playground
of a glossy coated bird.
Ibis is his name.

Fishes unaware
of close lurking danger
in the sun-lit pond,

graze the bottom
like hungry cows unleashed
in a spring meadow.

In mechanic ways,
a sharp-hooked beak ploughs the earth
in search for easy prey.

A sudden darkening,
a shadow turns the water black
like a daytime eclipse.

Panic stricken fish
hiding between reed and stone
fleeing for dear life.

## Summary

The feathery kiss
of summer breeze
on my naked arms
fills my heart
with tenderness
awakening sudden warmth.
Overcome by consciousness
no soul can do me harm.
The power of this subtle geste
creating wordless charm
is all you need for happiness
awareness closing in.
The wonder of nature's touch
is just a shiver on your skin.

### Turn my back

I wish I were invisible
among the gruelling crowd
but yet endowed with power
forcing their eyes to the ground.
Be anonymous,
mirroring their moods,
reflecting back to them
the destruction of their minds.
Be a stranger
in the sterile streets
walking tall and free
under unforgiving skies.
Be my own fascination
choose my exile in isolation,
amputated and severed
from the hostile kind.

**For my brown friends**


Child of Masters and Slaves
your name came down
with the wind of the Icy North,
the tone of your skin
on the ride of African waves.
You carry the history
of the tiny land,
the fathers of the trade
heading for an ancient land
took your mother as a maid.
Where do you belong
heir of this painful past?
Who dare trample you
until this day
and call you just half-cast?
It is not your fault
you are not to blame.
Down with the submissive stand,
raise your voice,
put your claim,
on a future without chain.

### That is how we are

Trust is broken,
hearts are down,
prejudice has spoken,
ego lost its crown.

Perception, nasty lie,
keeps haunting us all,
we scream and cry,
when we stumble and fall.

Eyes, the very mirror of our soul
do not often speak the truth,
playing their doubtful role,
adding to our bruise.

We swallow our pride,
we digest the hurt
until the burden turns light
as the flight of a bird.

We bend like a reed,
it sounds bizarre,
the pain will recede,
but we stay who we are.

This is our life,
this is our way,
we struggle and strive,
humans we stay.

Making love or war all over again,
we sing and pray,
this is life of man
until his dying day.

### The Paradise Widowbird

On the Highveld
where the sky is low,
I saw a Paradise widowbird
carrying his heavy load.
The burden of his useless tail
preventing him from flight,
only serves his vanity,
reflected in the female eye.
Hovering against the wind,
his flag trailing behind,
turning  him into easy prey,
for the ever hunting kite.
I pity this poor beauty,
trapped in his summer jail.
He only be released
from this ostentatious play
when the wind gets cold
and the land turns damp
and winter is on its way.
Invisible, unmarked he'll be,
shedding his display.
He'll take to the sky again
jubilant and free,
until the call of spring
will wake the urge
to stand his ground
and impress a mate.
Boasting the longest tail
and the blackest coat,
voluntarily he surrenders,
offering himself for sale,
sealing his fate,
in a shameless tender.

## Spiritual energy

Words of wise men,
heal my soul,
rock my mind
reverse my goal.
But false prophets,
building institutes
with lust of power,
severe me from my roots.
They will not get a hold on me,
I'm averse of dogma and taboos,
the self proclaimed correct
in the end, will make you lose.
They lure you into loyalty,
for your sake they pray
to further their own purpose,
on your integrity they prey.
I cherish my own conscience,
let me speak out loud:
Choosing between good and bad
is what it is all about.
My independent mind
travels a pot-holed road,
alone in the wilderness
carrying my unshared load,
will ultimately discover
the energy and light,
the comfort of the universe
shining strong and bright,
the sense of belonging
connection with the past,
there is no time or space
nor limits that will last.
The eternal cycle
will always be around
call it Nature, call it God,
Dance to the rhythm of its sound.

## Witbank

The black monster emerging
amidst banks of soot laden mist,
vomits ever burning flames
rising like an iron fist.
Challenging the sky
with its poisonous release
threatening our very lives
with pollution and disease.
Filled with unleashed anger,
fuming and enraged
consuming all our oxygen,
untamed and uncaged.
For the sake of energy,
our ever demanding greed,
to save our economy,
our families to feed.
Blurring our vision,
it is a glimpse of hell,
suffocating us conscientiously
with a nauseating smell.
Thousands of strong young men
go to work every day
to feed the monsters mouth with coal
in a never ending way.
The place they live is "Schoongezicht",
whoever did invent this name,
must have been from older times
or was otherwise insane.
The elephant once did roam
in this God forsaken place.
The river then full of life
is now a hopeless case.
There is no water anymore,
pitch black banks is all there is left,
with undiluted acid,
leaving the old riverbed naked and bereft.

In the veld, the open mine
colours our future black.
People will see no long term gain
only a setback.
For greedy and the businessmen,
energy brings wealth,
but ultimately they will lose out
paying with their health
Let us not create another hell
Prevent us from this beast
This is no sustainability
but just a short lived feast.

## Prayer for a brown mother

Do not feel hurt.
Push aside your anger,
Create room to face the other.
Not into aggression be lured,
Invoke the protection
of your sister and your brother.
Hide from those who cast a spell
of doom and frustration
provoking you to drink,
from the poisonous well
of bitterness and pride
bringing you to the very brink.
Exposing you to its malodorous stench
of accusations and deceptions
of self-pity and victimhood
of bitterness and revenge.
Find your identity, your dignity
Find your root.
Do no point the finger
Do no throw the blame
Heal yourself, forgive the other.
Do not in the past linger
Turn your face towards the light
Who else could do it than a mother?

## Mother sea

As a child,
I adored the sea
as a power of creation.
I watched her
coming for me
in my ignited imagination.
Off shore
she took me
in her cradling arms,
around the world
with the winds of trade
to icy colds and tropical warmth.
Returning me softly
to the golden island
lined with dunes.
My body stood
as an Aeolian harp
playing global tunes.
Praising her devotedly
for the blessings
of the earth,
breathing life
into particles
able to give birth.
One day,
she will come again
and take my tired heart.
to that ongoing eternity,
from which
I'm an integral part.

## My brain

My brain is a universe
with stars, a moon, a sun,
a cosmic constellation
in cycles it does run.

My brain is a tree
branching wide and high
with roots, leaves and bark
reaching for the sky.

My brain is a river
meandering down low
with creeks, lakes and channels
in a constant flow.

My brain is a coral reef
with layers of fine lace
and hollows full of life
lost in an endless maze.

My brain is my energy
the fuel and the source
of action and creativity,
my magical force.

## Moonscape (Namibia)

Wrapped in my weariness,
I walk the moon-like scape.
On the sands my tired steps,
commit a brutal rape.
My soul matches a specie
of the oldest plants:
Welwitschia Mirabilis
only grows in Namib sands.
My thirsty skin,
like mud-caked earth
yearning for the summer rain
screams a shrivelled curse.
What should I learn from this hostile place
where no tree meets the eye,
where only death seems to
loom under hellish skies?
I see crickets erecting shields
in splendid efficiency
catching every drop of dew
coming from the nearby sea.
Even springbok stay alive
where desert's wind blows
only eating scrub's tender shoots
to not impede its growth.
Black-backed jackals
and the brown hyena
scramble for food
in this sandy arena.
Life saving succulents
providing water, food,
its flowers turning in due time
into nutritious fruit.
To see nature's power,
open up your rigid mind
invigorate your sceptic soul
leaving fear behind.

### Nandi, the spotted eagle owl

Noiseless,
you flew into my memory
your big wings spread.
Self assured
with a mouse in your beak
you settled on my bed.
I knew you were coming,
I was waiting for you,
emotion rising in my throat.
Offering me food,
I thanked you,
stroking your spotted coat.
I felt a great wonder,
both tenderness and pain
in this mutual connection.
I knew it would pass,
this magical moment,
single token of animal affection.

## Once I was African

Once I was African
walking Laetoli steps
along slopes of volcanoes
above vertiginous depths,
following the tracks
of migrating herds,
searching the sky
for scavenging birds,
living in cruel harmony
with my fellow creatures,
wind, sun and rain
shaping my special features.
My children walked out on me
in evolutionary mutation
displaying their art
of awesome adaptation.
In our communal sky
there only is diversity, no race,
once we all were African
sharing the same space.

*Laetoli, Tanzania, the place where footprints were found of early hominids.

## The search

Tracking my past
along the dusty road
of fading memories,
peeling of layers of
solidified pain,
annihilating feelings that linger
with unbearable tenacity,
trying to loosen the grip,
digging in the hollows
of my brain,
searching for the core,
the diamond in deposit
waiting inside of me.

## Malian Music

Unquenchable yearning
moving my soul,
I sleepwalk in my dreams
to the rhythm of your sound
following the pied piper tones
of your griot high priests:
Ousmane,Oumou,Djelimane,
Mory,Ali Farka, Salif,
Habib, Rokia, Toumani,
Miryam and Amadou.
We sat together and played,
one space, one time,
we were one rising,
in waves of enchantment
beyond all differences,
colour, culture, age,
accompanied
by pangs of nostalgia,
lost in time.

## Counting blessings

Driving along the Corniche
not yet ten
with my father,
at my right hand side
the restless grey North Sea,
Western winds blowing
down the boulevard of Scheveningen,
waves splashing on the pier
we sing Dutch tunes
I count my blessings.
Driving along the Corniche
not yet twenty
with my boy friend,
at my right hand side
the luxuriant Mediterranean sea
Mistral blowing
from Cap d'Ail to Ventimiglia
bougainvillea hanging from the cliff
we sing French chansons
I count my blessings.
Driving along the Corniche
not yet thirty
with my newlywed husband,
at my right hand side
the thousand and one night Red Sea,
Djibouti dhow winds blowing
along the sea drive of Hodeidah
eyes behind Ottoman shutters,
we sing Yemeni rhythms
I count my blessings.

Driving along the Corniche
not yet forty
with my young son,
at my right hand side
the malachite Indian Ocean
Trade winds blowing
from Masasani to Dar
Mwalimu's* peacocks screaming
we sing Tanzanian songs
I count my blessings.
Driving along the Corniche
not yet fifty
with my little girl,
at my right hand side
the cobalt cold Atlantic Ocean
Harmattan blowing
from Dakar to Nianing
baobabs standing guard
we sing Mande tributes
I count my blessings.
Driving along the Corniche
not yet old
with my true love,
at my right hand side
cold Benguela meets warm Indian
South Easterly blowing
from Cape town to Chapman's peak
sea lions basking on boulders
we sing South African harmonies
I count my blessings.

*Mwalimu - Julius Nyerere

Sepl
aquarelle on silk

# The homecoming

I cherish my nomad life
but I can't bear
the sadness in your eyes
every time I leave you,
one of so many goodbyes.
You stand at the door,
I push you aside
and when I close up,
I take away your light.
Whiffs of your smell
accompany me
and linger in my nose.
Awareness of love
smells better than a rose.
When the days go by
I forget
how you look when you run
your energy, your coat
shining in the sun.
Then I come back,
your frantic embrace,
your jumping and leaping
that feast of recognition
makes me feel like weeping.
You are so blessed
not knowing
the pain of missing,
I cannot avoid
your doggish kissing.
Excitedly barking,
you sweep me of my feet
for a homecoming celebration,
back is your memory
by sheer association.

## Vicky's messenger

A fancy dressed bird*
in yellow and red
adorned with white pearls
and black spots
woke me from my tormented bed.
It's alarm-clock song
in my ear was ringing,
wake up,
wipe your tears,
Vicky's messenger is singing.
Into my room he peered
in the morning light
and made me smile,
my heart was tuned,
everything turned bright.
His message was clear,
didn't need words,
you are one she'll remember,
when you need her,
just watch the birds.

*the crested barbet

## The whale

When I watched the birds
I saw a whale pass
ploughing through the water
propelling its big mass,
exchanging its arctic feeding grounds
for the summer romance place,
whistling mating songs
across the blue green bays.
Gentle giants, close to the touch
in mutual curiosity,
presenting themselves
with humble generosity,
in spite of us destroying them
although we are no match
with our advanced technology
they remain an easy catch.
How to prevent this crime
against this ancient beauty
and instil respect
to honour our duty
towards those who chose
the prolific sea, our brothers
within evolution's extended family,
our common ancestry.
We, being with so many,
we invade his space
if we don't protect him,
we soon will count his days.

# Kelp

In parallel perfection,
a water ballet's synchronicity,
through narrow gullies
stems of kelp snake their way,
on and on, a dance
of lethal attraction
on the road
to death and decay.
Giant seaweed
like so many placentas
torn from the womb of the sea,
between glowing yellow stones,
their rubbery wrappings
adorning the shore,
as the sea, moving to and fro,
gently moans.
The salty tomb of afterbirth,
like felt trees
upside down,
the cradle of tiny life.
On nature's dinner table:
insects and crustaceans,
a decadent meal,
on which scavenging seagulls thrive.

The Owlet
(clay / pottery)

### The best days of our life

Remember how we swam
with the horses
in the Mediterranean sea,
running them dry
down the beach
their manes flowing free.
Salt crystals
clinging to our bodies
shining like diamonds
in the sun,
the best days of our life
we guessed,
had just begun.
Lying in the stables
wrapped in
their body heat,
listening to
their breathing
the stamping of their feet.
Those days among
the steaming fields
covered in thick reed,
white egrets hovering above
as far as the eye could meet.
Kingfishers, blue jewels
splashing to the water
in a sea of green,
hunting for the tiniest fish
you had ever seen.
Remember how
this was so much part of us
coming to the core
of what happiness could be,
expanding our consciousness,
dreams couldn't flee.

Easy was our life
back then,
our minds
in peace , at rest,
until the autumn came
to remind us
that it wouldn't last.

## Glamorous

You are so glamorous,
you are so chic
said the socialite to me
said I: I'm not
what I appear to be.
But you do look glamorous,
you do look chic
said the socialite to me.
Said I: Look here, I'm not
I play music and write poetry.
Still, that is glamorous,
that is so chic
said the socialite to me.
Said I: Stop it,
I don't want to be.
Why not glamorous,
why not chic?
said the socialite to me.
Said I: Do you sell something?
What do you want from me?
Your house must be glamorous,
your house must be chic
said the socialite to me.
Said I: I am not rich
I am not high society.
But your friend is glamorous
your friend is chic
said the socialite to me.
Said I: Maybe,
but she is not to me.
How can she not be glamorous,
how can she not be chic?
said the socialite to me.

Said I: leave us alone
she is just like me.
That is not glamorous,
that is not chic
said the socialite to me.
Said I: so it is,
you made an enemy.

## The Streets of Bamako

Did you ever hear
a horse scream?
No, you can't have,
horses don't scream,
they suffer in silence
the beatings of life
on the streets of Bamako.
One wheel in the gutter,
a man beats and beats
the life out of the horse.
The man is no beast though,
the horse falls on his knees
in a last prayer,
on the streets of Bamako.
The ribs of the horse
stick out of his skin.
He is the breadwinner,
he is the livelihood
of the man
dressed in his poverty
on the streets of Bamako.
The man beats
the rhythm of frustration
as he beats his wife,
his children
and his dog
out of sheer desperation
on the streets of Bamako.
A projection out of anger,
out of lack of power
out of lack of identity
the man screams inside
silently
like the horse
on the streets of Bamako.

The horse lies lifeless
on his side,
his mouth is bleeding.
The butchers come around
and roast him
on the charcoal fires
on the streets of Bamako.

**Let me introduce**


She is a child of Christmas Eve
born between the rubble of the war.
In the hall, voices
singing Christmas carols
seeping through the door.
Little Mary she was named
appropriate for that day.
Nurses in white uniforms
for her life did pray.
Child of winter, child of cold
yearning for the sun,
to the heart of old Gondwana
she did run.
The cradle of human kind
is where she longed to be.
Africa's ancient call
seemed to be her destiny....

Gondwana: the southernmost supercontinent 200 million years ago

## Loss and gain (on leaving South Africa)

I watch my images
in pain
where I used to watch
in anticipation.
But so it was every time
of loss and gain
a tender sprouting
and  then consolidation.
Being torn up,
I can't refrain
my nostalgic tears
of desperation.
I cannot keep
my hope is vain
I cannot hold
there is no consolation.
Loss cuts deep
but it will drain
through the channels
of new expectation.

## My soul wanted to sneak out

In the middle of the night
I woke up
and saw my soul
standing next to my bed.
I cried out for him
not to leave me
but I was powerless
paralysed and mute.
I panicked and
tried to tell him
not to go, that
I was not whole
without him.
But he looked
in disdain and
had wanted
to sneak out on me
without being noticed
as if he was going
secretly to a party.
I felt like a mother
refraining him
from pleasure.
There was no need
for my soul to
sneak out like that
there is still
too much to do.
I couldn't miss him yet.
Then I remembered
my brain, the tool
of command,

my remote control
and I urged my soul
to come back
and merge again
with my material body
to feel whole again
and beloved
and write down
my experience
and he did,
so relieved I was.
What would have happened
if he wouldn't have?
Would I die?

## Lost paradise

Poor Perlemoen
lying on your back
on the blinding sand,
your mother of pearl
inside shining,
your pastel palette
showing.
Poor people scavenged
your soft insides
for the rich men's table,
left your remains
in this cemetery
of cruel beauty
on the shores
of the turquoise sea.
Abelone, heavenly name
of a lost paradise.
Why do you have to pay
for your sluggish ways?

# Contents

Demer Press, ePublisher, Belgium


*Parchment, Testament*, poems by Joris Iven (translator: John Irons), 2008
*Lakes and Gardens*, poems by Hannie Rouweler (translators: John Irons and Hannie Rouweler), 2008
*Mirrors and Deserts/Spiegels en Woestijnen*, bilingual, English/Dutch, poems by Anise Koltz and Margalit Matitiahu (translator: Hannie Rouweler), 2008, 2010
*Anniversary Dinner Robert Burns, My love is like a red, red rose*, bilingual, Dutch/English, poems by Joris Iven (translator: John Irons), January 2009
*De voorvaderen en de heilige berg/The ancestors and the sacred mountain*, poems by Mazisi Kunene, ZULU POEMS, bilingual, English/Dutch (translator poems: Joris Iven; translator Epilogue and Interview: John Irons), 2009
Hommage aan de schilder Tony Mafia/A tribute to the painter Tony Mafia, *BLACK SUN*, bilingual, Dutch/English, 10 poems/10 poets from The Netherlands and Belgium (translators: John Irons and Annmarie Sauer), 2009
*Moving Spots*, poems by Hannie Rouweler (translators: John Irons and Hannie Rouweler), 2009
*Love as Flowers*, poems by Stella Evelyne Tesha, 2009
*Mooie rode zijden liefde/Beautiful red silk love*, bilingual, English/Dutch, poems by Pearse Hutchinson (translators: Joris Iven and Peter Flynn), 2010
*Beroemde Chagga verhalen/Famous Chagga stories*, bilingual, English/Dutch, stories by O. Mtuweta H. Tesha (translator: Melissa Yvonne Tesha; co-translator Hannie Rouweler), 2010
*Poppies and Chamber Music*, Ten poets from The Netherlands and Flanders, editors: Thierry Deleu and Hannie Rouweler (translator: John Irons), 2010
*A splendid view on words*, poems by Willem M. Roggeman (translators a.o. Susan and Roy Eales), 2010
*Voices from Everywhere*, international poets, editors: Mark Walmsley and Hannie Rouweler, 2011
*Enlightened from inside out*, Poems and Art, editors: Roger Nupie and Hannie Rouweler (translator: John Irons), 2011
*Blue Ribbons*, poems by Floris Brown, 2011
*About everything that is not right*, Protest Poems, international poets, 2011
*Heartscapes*, poems by Marion de Vos, 2011


website: www.demerpress.be
e-address: info@demerpress.be

CPSIA information can be obtained at www.ICGtesting.com
Printed in the USA
LVOW122351260911

247957LV00001B/6/P